little book of

LONDON
style

Published in 2022 by Welbeck
An imprint of Welbeck Non-Fiction Limited,
part of Welbeck Publishing Group.

Based in London and Sydney
www.welbeckpublishing.com

ISBN 978-1-80279-274-4

Printed in Dubai

10 9 8 7 6 5 4 3 2

KAREN HOMER

little book of

LONDON
style

The Fashion Story of the Iconic City

WELBECK

CONTENTS

introduction page 6

iNTRODUCTiON

"There's nowhere else like London. Nothing at all, anywhere."
Vivienne Westwood

London is without doubt one of the style capitals of the world, ever since the 1960s and the arrival of the miniskirt, and the young and fashionable began to flock to the King's Road and Carnaby Street to pick up the latest fashions.

Thanks to its vibrant youth culture, London has seen some of the most recognizable fashion subcultures take root on its streets. From Teddy boys and mods and rockers through to punks, New Romantics and goths, the city has always welcomed self-expression through clothes. A lively club culture has also contributed to many fashion trends, from the visually stunning BodyMap designs to the neon-bright rave scene.

The city has of course produced some of the world's most famous fashion designers. Mary Quant was one of the first to embrace affordable fashion for the masses, along with Barbara Hulanicki, founder of iconic store Biba. Then came Vivienne Westwood, who, with partner Malcolm McLaren and his band the Sex Pistols, sparked the punk fashion scene. And Westwood was not the only one who realized the power

Introduction

A model poses by the traffic lights as an iconic red London bus speeds past. Photographed for *Vogue* by Norman Parkinson, 1960.

KEEP
LEFT

of fashion and what a radical slogan emblazoned across the chest could achieve: Katharine Hamnett made fashion firmly political in the 1980s, even meeting Margaret Thatcher wearing an anti-nuclear war T-shirt.

The sheer volume of talent that has come out of London's Central Saint Martins college of fashion is phenomenal. A hugely creative couturier, the inimitable John Galliano was one of the first in the mid-1980s, followed soon after by the legendary Alexander McQueen, who was arguably the most important fashion designer of his generation. Stella McCartney is another of the alumni who have become international players, along with the likes of Hussein Chalayan, Gareth Pugh, Ashish Gupta and Christopher Kane – all of whom have cemented London's reputation for avant-garde fashion.

London also has a long tradition of style icons that the rest of the world emulate, from the classic style of Princess Diana to models such as Twiggy and Jean Shrimpton, Kate Moss, Naomi Campbell and Alexa Chung. British musicians have also had a big influence on the world of style, with artists as varied as David Bowie, the Beatles and the Rolling Stones, Siouxsie Sioux, Sade and Harry Styles, all pushing boundaries.

The home, along with Paris, Milan and New York, to one of the big four fashion weeks, London is also the most egalitarian of fashion destinations. It isn't just celebrities, models and designers who inspire – London has always attracted attention for its street style, seen as the most exciting and eclectic in the world.

This 1963 shot by Norman Parkinson shows British models Melanie Hampshire and Jill Kennington flanked by two policemen. The pair are both wearing Mary Quant striped wool dresses.

chapter 1

BIRTH OF A STYLE CAPITAL

FASHION FREEDOM

After the First World War, London began to emerge as one of the style capitals of the world as women broke free from their corsets and the long-fought suffragettes' battle triumphed, with more than eight million women being given the right to vote. The activists proudly displayed their colours of purple, green and white, choosing looser, more functional clothes over cripplingly restrictive dresses. While it might take another decade for all women to achieve the vote, or even dare to wear trousers, the seeds that allowed women to express their liberation through fashion had been sown.

The so-called Roaring Twenties saw the emergence of the flapper movement, with its beaded sheath dresses stopping daringly just below the knee. The city's bright young things, their hair newly bobbed, lived a hedonistic nocturnal life in the cocktail bars and jazz clubs of London's Trocadero. At the Kit-Kat club on the Haymarket, reputedly Europe's most decadent and expensive nightclub, they rubbed shoulders with the playboy Prince of Wales. The following day they would emerge bleary-eyed just in time for a smart lunch – dressed in a tailored skirt suit, topped with an oversized fur coat and cloche hat, a style of daywear as extravagant as their post-war lifestyle.

The more daring women of the 1920s experimented with the new vogue for mannish trousers, inspired by Coco Chanel. The French designer's affair with the immensely wealthy Duke of Westminster saw her spend summers at his Scottish

Coco Chanel with her aristocratic lover the Duke of Westminster in 1924. His traditional English attire inspired many of the French fashion designer's creations.

Princess Elizabeth (left), as she then was, wearing
her regulation Auxiliary Territorial Service boiler suit
during her training as a driver and mechanic.

estate, often borrowing his tweed shooting jacket and flannel trousers, an aristocratic British style that informed her own designs. While London style generally had a smarter feel, the country look influenced fashion and it wasn't uncommon to see women in a pair of Oxford bags that rivalled the 1970s for their volume.

During the 1930s London remained a vibrant and fashionable city. Unlike in the United States, where the effects of the Great Depression decimated the fortunes of so many socialites, London kept on partying, dressing up for the many dinner dances and clubs. With Parisian designers like Coco Channel and Madeleine Vionnet dictating fashion, London society women slavishly followed current trends as hemlines dropped and the decade's iconic bias-cut, figure-hugging silk gown appeared. Fur remained hugely popular, trimming hats, coats and gloves, and it would be decades before anyone questioned fashion's exploitation of animals.

Towards the end of the 1930s, as war once again approached, the fashion landscape of London changed. Until now the luxury of dressing in the latest styles had been the preserve of the wealthy. The most famous British fashion designer at the time was Norman Hartnell, who dressed many members of the aristocracy including the Queen and her daughter, Princess Elizabeth, as well as style icons such as Wallis Simpson. But as men went off to war and women rose to the challenge of working en masse in jobs as varied as factory work and farming, their clothes adapted accordingly. Practical trousers replaced skirts, and the memorable Land Girl jumpsuit, accessorized with a headscarf, remains a popular vintage look to this day. Even Princess Elizabeth, as she was then, appeared in photographs dressed in her regulation boiler suit to carry out her work in the Auxiliary Territorial Service.

Birth of a Style Capital

Although a certain militarization had already crept into fashion, with squared-off shoulders and sensible knee-length skirts replacing the long draped elegance of the 1930s, it was clothes rationing, which lasted from 1941 until 1949, that had the biggest effect on London style. Socialites and housewives alike were suddenly at the mercy of what their coupon book could buy them, with less well-off women left to buy cheap fabrics that quickly wore out. To combat the problem of poor-quality clothing, the UK government devised the utility clothing scheme which, under the CC41 label, regulated the mass production of clothes at controlled prices.

In a stroke of genius, a scheme was devised to invite the top London fashion designers, including Norman Hartnell and Hardy Amies, to create clothes that would best make use of the fabric available. As fashion historian Jayne Shrimpton pointed out in *Fashion in the 1940s*, the initiative "...might never have succeeded had the government not taken the inspired decision to involve leading London couturiers in the design of Utility Clothing."

With the cachet of his royal connections, the outfits that Hartnell in particular designed became immensely popular. Dresses had simple, elegant lines and minimal embellishment, skirts were knee-length and pleated, and jackets maintained the fashionable boxy silhouette of the era. These were clothes that for the first time made fashion universal for all British women.

Towards the end of the 1940s, however, people became tired of clothes rationing and looked across the English Channel to the exciting new fashions emerging from Paris, notably those created by a designer named Christian Dior.

In February 1947 Christian Dior released his debut collection appropriately dubbed the New Look. The suits, with their

In 1942, models showcase outfits created by Norman Hartnell as part of the utility fashion initiative. The clothes were designed to make the best use of rationed fabric yet were surprisingly stylish.

immensely full skirts and elegant tailored jackets, nipped in to accentuate the hourglass figure, seemed like a dream to Londoners still wearing pared-back Utility clothing, but that didn't stop Dior showing his collection at the Savoy hotel in front of a mesmerized audience. As a confirmed Anglophile, Dior once said of English women: "I find them amongst the most beautiful and distinguished in the world." The designer also greatly admired the British tradition of quality fabric

Birth of a Style Capital

Princess Margaret was a fan and muse of French
fashion designer and Anglophile Christian Dior.

making, especially the use of tweeds and other woollens. Amongst Dior's fans was Princess Margaret: she became a muse to the French designer, who described her as "…a real fairy princess, delicate, graceful, exquisite."

What few people realized, however, was that Dior himself had been influenced by British designer Norman Hartnell, even writing in a letter to his English counterpart: "It was the crinolines you designed for the Queen [Mother] to wear to Paris in 1939 which inspired my evening dresses and the New Look."

Hartnell had also attempted to revive his full-skirted silhouette in 1946, a year before Dior's New Look, but with fabric rationing still in full force was unable to. Hartnell was, however, commissioned to design Princess Elizabeth's wedding dress and trousseau for her marriage to Prince Philip in November 1947. Given an extra 200 clothing coupons by the British government, the gown was a triumph with its full skirt embroidered with thousands of seed-pearls and white beads. British women began to feel inspired by fashion once again.

London style during the 1950s slowly began to embrace the post-war luxury allowed by increased fabric production. As men came back from war, women were encouraged to return to the home. An emphasis on an ultra-feminine silhouette contrasted with the utilitarian designs of the previous decade: full-skirted dresses and heels were accessorized with ladylike gloves and hats and, of course, the seamed nylon stockings that had become popular a few years earlier.

But among London teenagers came a swelling wave of alternative fashion strongly associated with the new rock'n'roll music emerging from the United States. Teddy boys, as they became known, were London's first fashion subculture, and with the new decade the speed of changing fashions picked up as London entered the Swinging Sixties.

Birth of a Style Capital

chapter 2

FASHION DESIGNERS

1960s:
THE SWINGING SIXTIES

Mary Quant

With her trademark Vidal Sassoon five-point bob and buttock-skimming hemlines, Mary Quant was the first designer to offer youthful fashions to the masses, and in doing so put London firmly on the fashion map. A graduate in illustration from Goldsmiths' College, Quant was a self-taught fashion designer who in 1955 opened her first shop, Bazaar, at 138a King's Road.

An early adherent of the Chelsea beatnik set and its monochrome look, which drew on Italian sportswear and the clean, functional lines beloved of dancers, Quant wanted "relaxed clothes suited to the actions of normal life." Her goal was female emancipation through fashion and, unlike the more established fashion designers of the time, she was creating clothes for her contemporaries and wearing them herself.

In the early years of Bazaar, Quant adopted an extraordinary knife-edge business model where the sales from the day at the shop went to buy fabric that was then turned into new stock overnight. Despite the stressful cycle of constant production, Quant realized that by working in this way she could constantly offer her customers something new and exciting

Fashion Designers

Mary Quant wearing one of her iconic minidresses, pictured in her London studio in 1966.

Mary Quant created a whole lifestyle, including accessories and
a make-up range in the same vibrant colours as her fashions.

at competitive prices thanks to little wastage or overheads.
Consequently, Bazaar always had the freshest and most
exciting looks available, and the young flocked to buy them.

Along with the lure of the new, Mary Quant's other unique
selling point was that, for the first time, Londoners were
being offered fashion that wasn't just a replica of what older
generations were wearing. Often credited with inventing
the miniskirt, Quant created bold, unapologetic outfits
such as tunic dresses paired with brightly coloured tights,

Fashion Designers

and twisted traditional garments like men's cardigans into dresses. Her clothes were popularized by the first supermodels, including Twiggy, whose ultra-lean physique perfectly suited the barely-there dresses.

Quant was an innovator too, who drew on the past to reinvent it as subversive new fashion. Her use of modern materials was also pioneering, with plastic collars a mainstay of her dresses, and she became the first designer to use PVC to create wet-look clothing.

> ## "Fashion is a tool to compete in life outside the home"
> *Mary Quant*

Perhaps Quant's greatest achievement, and one which had such an impact in both London and beyond, was to democratize fashion. Her price points were low enough that a humble secretary could afford them. During the early 1960s her business expanded globally, bringing London's iconic look to the United States through a contract with chain store JCPenney. It wasn't just clothes that Quant offered, either. Her influence extended to make-up – her famously vibrant "paintbox" range perfectly complemented her fashions – along with her trademark bright hosiery and playful plastic jewellery. Young girls could even buy their very own "Daisy Fashion Doll" complete with miniature versions of Quant's real-life fashions.

Towards the end of the 1960s Mary Quant continued to push fashion boundaries with the introduction of hot pants, a style, she claimed, "sold faster than [we] could make them," but it will always be the controversial miniskirt with which she is most associated.

Biba / Barbara Hulanicki

Mention 1960s fashion shops and the place that immediately springs to mind is Biba, with its multitude of exotic designs. The label was founded by Polish-born Barbara Hulanicki, a Brighton College of Art graduate and fashion illustrator, who once said: "In England, we were thought to be the worst-dressed people in Europe."

Hulanicki is generally seen as one of the cornerstones of the "mod" fashion movement of the 1960s, but she was equally inspired by the romantic Pre-Raphaelite era, its influence reflected in the muted tones in her designs.

At first, Hulanicki's clothes were supplied by mail-order only, allowing a wide range of designs to be trialled without risk. The first notable success was a pink gingham, sleeveless shift dress with a matching headscarf, which closely resembled an outfit worn by Brigitte Bardot. After being featured in the *Daily Mirror*, the dress, which Hulanicki had expected would sell around 3,000 items, was ordered more than 17,000 times, allowing the designer to open the first of her iconic stores on Abingdon Road in Kensington in 1964.

As with Mary Quant, Biba's short dresses were suited to the skinny physiques that 1960s women aspired to. Hulanicki's sleeves were famously narrow, so much so that you could barely bend your arms, yet they became a signature of many of her designs. Colours were dark and mysterious in an autumnal palette of burgundy, rusty orange and plum, and her famous bruised purple and accents of gold and silver added a touch of Hollywood glamour. As the 1960s drew to

Fashion Designers

Biba mail order catalogue, c. 1967. This rayon suit was available with either trousers or a miniskirt.

Twiggy photographed by Justin de Villeneuve at Biba, 1971.

a close Biba embraced what we now see as a classic 1970s silhouette, which included flared jumpsuits, platform heels and large floppy hats.

Biba sought to keep prices affordable, attracting teenagers and London office girls who were desperate to keep up with current fashions and happy to buy new outfits frequently. As a result, Hulanicki is often credited with bringing youthful fashions to the high street. Biba grew rapidly during the early 1970s, opening their famous seven-storey store, Big Biba, in 1974. A lifestyle destination, it included an art gallery, bookshop and foodhall, but the expansion was nevertheless a risk, which Hulanicki acknowledged when she said: "Every time I went into the shop, I was afraid it would be for the last time." Her fears were not unfounded: a year later the company went bust, but Biba's reputation remains legendary.

Fashion Designers

Barbara Hulanicki poses with her husband Stephen Fitz-
Simon in the louche interior of her Biba store, *c.*1975.

Jean Muir

Among the social and aesthetic revolution happening in London during the 1960s Jean Muir offered a sharp contrast to the youthful mass-market designs of Mary Quant and Biba. The London-born designer, who as a child already showed a prodigious talent for sewing, went straight from leaving school to a job at famous London store Liberty. With her natural flair, Muir soon worked her way up from salesgirl to become part of the design illustration team for its ready-to-wear department. After leaving Liberty she spent a brief time at Jaeger before launching her first label, Jane & Jane, where her elegant creations in Liberty-print silk won several awards.

In 1966 Muir launched her eponymous label and continued to create classic garments in luxurious fabrics aimed at women of all ages who wanted a timeless look. Her signature wool crêpe dresses and soft suede and leather coats revealed a quality of craftsmanship more often associated with the couture houses of Paris, and her sense of form and the fluid lines of her garments was masterful. Muir's clothes are often remembered for being dark and sombre, but her understanding of colour was superb. She demanded absolute perfection from her fabric dyers, with whom she worked closely to create a palette of deep blues and greens so dark they were almost black, yet there were always accents of intense orange or yellow to punctuate her collections. Embellishments to her clothes were few and far between and were either functional, such as carefully placed buttons, or took the form of a single decorative touch to a garment such as pin-tucking.

Muir consciously rejected high fashion and the looks expressed by the decade's youthful subcultures, instead focusing on restraint and elegance. Yet, despite her relative austerity, she is to this day widely admired as a designer.

Designer Jean Muir photographed in 1965 wearing one of her
own classically designed, yet still fashionable dresses.

1970s / 1980s:

FLOWER POWER TO SHOULDER PADS

Ossie Clark and Celia Birtwell

During a decade from the mid-1960s through to the arrival of Vivienne Westwood and punk rock, designer Ossie Clark and his textile artist wife Celia Birtwell ruled the London fashion scene; the pair's influence on global fashion would extend over the next four decades.

Rejecting the silhouette of the time, Clark famously derided the boyish physiques so popularized by the likes of model Twiggy, instead choosing to design for women of all shapes and sizes. As Celia Birtwell told the *Independent* on his death in 1996: "He had an extraordinary talent for cutting and could transform a thin person or a plump person into whatever shape they wanted to be."

Clark's romantic designs were a marked departure from the brightly coloured plastic dresses of Mary Quant or the uncomfortably skintight creations in scratchy fabrics made by Biba. Instead, he created figure-skimming gowns in delicate fabrics, crafting shapes that harked back to the 1930s and the golden age of Hollywood glamour. Finding inspiration in dance and ballet, Clark aimed to design free-flowing garments that graced and flattered the female form rather than trying to pretend it didn't exist.

Fashion Designers

A vibrant 1970s yellow and grey velvet coat by Ossie Clark and
Celia Birtwell featuring one of their typical prints, Candy Flower.

Clark first appeared on the fashion scene in 1964, making
clothes for designer Alice Pollock's boutique Quorum on the
King's Road, and in 1965 Birtwell started designing prints
for his garments. Birtwell's romantic patterns, inspired
by sources as varied as Vita Sackville-West's garden and
Impressionist painters, perfectly complemented Clark's
designs, which were further elevated out of the ordinary

This typical creation by the pair from 1968 exemplifies both
Ossie Clark's romantic free-flowing outfits, designed to flatter
the female form, and Celia Birtwell's eye-catching prints.

by his use of fluid silks or crêpe de Chine. These were far more sophisticated than many of the peasant-style dresses emerging out of the rising hippy movement; nevertheless, inspired by the Bloomsbury set, Birtwell's designs invoked just enough of the pastoral fantasy to capture the free-spirited fashion mood of the late 1960s and early 1970s.

> ## "What's wrong with the way women dress is that they don't know anything about their bodies."
> *Ossie Clark*

In 1967 Clark, the first British designer to use Black models on the catwalk, presented his debut fashion show at Chelsea Town Hall. The rich and famous flocked to buy his designs and also created stage costumes for artists as varied as Mick Jagger and Liza Minnelli. Ossie Clark and Celia Birtwell married in 1969, two years later becoming the subject of David Hockney's painting *Mr and Mrs Clark and Percy*. The couple had two sons but divorced in 1974 when Clark adopted an increasingly hedonistic lifestyle which, along with the financial difficulties faced by his business, led to the depression that would become a recurring theme throughout the rest of his life, which sadly was beset by tragedy. Long-time partner Nicholas Balaban died of AIDS in 1994 and Clark himself was stabbed to death in 1996 at the age of 54 by former lover Diego Cogolato, tragically at a time when the designer was finally beginning to resurrect his career.

Immediately after her divorce, Celia Birtwell left fashion in favour of teaching but returned to textile design in 1984, most recently collaborating with brands as varied as Uniqlo and Maison Valentino.

Fashion Designers

Laura Ashley

Another designer who embraced pastoral fantasy was the Welsh-born Laura Ashley. As an aspiring maker in the 1950s, Ashley had developed a passion for antique quilts and found inspiration in the delicate floral patterns they featured, which she recreated for her early designs.

Ashley explored and reinterpreted vintage patterns, printing her own fabric to create her trademark designs. During the mid-1960s her husband and business partner, Bernard, developed a flat-bed printing press that enabled Ashley to drastically increase her production. Opening her first London shop in 1968, the designer played on the nostalgia for a simpler, more wholesome life in the English countryside. Her long floral-print dresses with their bows and puffed sleeves fitted perfectly with the hippy vibe of the 1970s.

Laura's designs had a uniquely British aesthetic, but such was her success in capturing the mood of moment that the company soon expanded worldwide. In the 1980s, along with the requisite string of pearls and "pie-crust" frilled-collar blouse, a Laura Ashley floral print became inextricably linked to London's "Sloane Ranger" look, and above all to the young Princess Diana. The backlit, translucent skirt the 19-year-old wore in the world-famous shot that broke the news of her relationship to Prince Charles was one of her designs.

The company blossomed until the tragic sudden death of Laura from a brain haemorrhage aged 60. Nevertheless the heritage florals are still popular and classic designs are highly sought after vintage pieces.

Fashion Designers

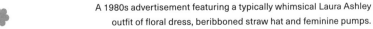

A 1980s advertisement featuring a typically whimsical Laura Ashley outfit of floral dress, beribboned straw hat and feminine pumps.

This extraordinary yellow dress was part of Zandra Rhodes's first solo collection, which was worn by actress Natalie Wood for an American *Vogue* shoot in 1970.

Zandra Rhodes

Instantly recognizable with her trademark bright pink bob, theatrical make-up and unapologetic dress sense, Zandra Rhodes exploded onto the London fashion scene during the 1970s. The daughter of a fitter at Charles Worth's haute couture house in Paris, fashion was in Rhodes's blood from the beginning. As a student of textile design, she cited influences including Andy Warhol, Roy Lichtenstein and Emilio Pucci, all lovers of bold graphics and bright colours.

During the late 1960s Rhodes's early designs were rejected by the conservative British fabric-printing industry as being too over the top, so the textile artist teamed up with her fellow Royal College of Art graduate, fashion designer Sylvia Ayton, to open a shop on the Fulham Road. Ayton's designs were made up in fabric by Rhodes, whose groundbreaking approach to fashion was evident in early experiments, including tattoo print transfers and paper dresses.

A year later Rhodes broke with Ayton to focus on her first solo collection. The voluminous yet graceful kaftan-like evening dresses reflected the popular early 1970s silhouette, but her colourful prints were unique. They were also timely as the fashion crowd started to reject Western materialism and explore other influences from around the globe, a trend she was also inspired by.

Always experimenting with scale and colour, Rhodes sewed her garments in such a way as to highlight portions of the print rather than cut a pattern from a continuous length of fabric. Constructed with clever use of layering and gathering and using techniques such as smocking and shirring, her dresses seemed to evolve organically into a selection of eye-catching feminine gowns, at once dramatic and elegant.

Fashion Designers

"To me colour gives confidence. It makes a strong statement: here I am, love me or hate me."
Zandra Rhodes

The extroverted designer credits Diana Vreeland with launching her into the mainstream, after the visionary editor of American *Vogue* dressed actress Natalie Wood for the magazine in Rhodes' first collection from 1970. As she explained to *Vogue* in 2016: "Diana Vreeland has been a great influence on me, as she encouraged and adored the way my prints were an integral part of the garments."

As her popularity grew, Rhodes opened her own London boutique and when punk arrived in the late 1970s the designer offered a unique twist on the trend, launching her 1977 Conceptual Chic collection. Included were slashed rayon dresses held together by ball-link chains and beaded safety pins, long before Versace recreated the idea. The designer has long been a favourite of celebrities and socialites, creating costumes for Freddie Mercury and Marc Bolan and evening dresses for Diana, Princess of Wales. A style icon, who was inextricably linked to the London fashion revolution of the 1970s, Rhodes continues to inspire a multitude of designers half a century later, recently creating a flamboyant homeware collection for IKEA.

Fashion Designers

Zandra Rhodes pictured in 1981 at a Woman of the Year lunch. The designer is instantly recognizable with her iconic bright pink hair, flamboyant make-up and glitzy outfit.

Vivienne Westwood

There is no fashion designer more linked to London's alternative fashion in the 1970s than Vivienne Westwood. Surprisingly, the doyenne of punk led a relatively conservative life in the early 1960s, married with a young son and working as a teacher, but the dissolution of her marriage and an introduction to a young art student changed her life for ever. As the designer explained to the *New York Times* in 1999: "I latched onto Malcolm [McLaren] as somebody who opened doors for me. I mean he seemed to know everything I needed at the time."

Quickly rejecting both the fashion and political status quo, Westwood started out making Teddy boy clothes for McLaren. In 1971 the pair opened their infamous shop Let It Rock, at 430 King's Road. The rock 'n' roll tribute store stocked zoot suits, brothel creepers and 1950s memorabilia. Soon Westwood started experimenting with her trademark punk rock look, customizing biker clothing to make leather jackets adorned with a multitude of zips worn over T-shirts featuring anti-capitalist slogans.

In 1975 the band the Sex Pistols, managed by McLaren, thrust punk into the limelight. Westwood's shop was given its most memorable moniker, SEX, and the designer used her association with the controversial band as a platform to explore even more anarchic fashion. The clothes were designed to aggressively shock, the complete opposite of the soft, free-flowing naturalistic fashions beloved of the hippies of the era. Almost all-black, with slashed layers thrown together from a mix of army surplus and second hand, the look radiated anger and discontent. Tight black trousers on both men and women were teamed with mohair sweaters and leather jackets, the look completed by heavy

Westwood and McLaren's notorious King's Road shop Sex was
famous for its punk and fetish wear. This image from 1976 sees
Vivienne Westwood joined by Steve Jones, regular customer
Danielle, Alan Jones, Chrissie Hynde and Jordan Mooney.

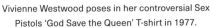

Vivienne Westwood poses in her controversial Sex
Pistols 'God Save the Queen' T-shirt in 1977.

A shot from Vivienne Westwood and Malcolm
McLaren's debut fashion show Pirate in 1981.

Doc Marten boots. Female punks wore miniskirts, fishnets
and stilettos; fetishistic sex bubbled barely below the surface
with bondage-style trousers and clothes made from PVC and
rubber. Adaptations like seams that unzipped at the crotch
and removable bum flaps accentuated the sexualized nature
of the clothing.

Customization was essential and punks splashed their leather
jackets with painted slogans and icons, adding metal chains,
studs, safety pins and even razor blades for a fiercer look.

Fashion Designers

Nothing was too much, even obscene imagery and Nazi motifs. To complete the image, hair was shaved and gelled into spikes, faces were whitened with contrasting black eyes and lips, and adorned with piercings. The establishment was incensed and a 1975 graphic T-shirt featuring two cowboys touching penises led to the arrest of a shop attendant, but the controversy only made punk more appealing.

As with many alternative fashions that initially blow up the sartorial landscape, a less threatening version of punk was gradually adopted by the mainstream. In 1978 the Sex Pistols split up and Westwood became increasingly disillusioned. Drawing on a long-time love of seventeenth- and eighteenth-century clothing – a style that again saw Westwood influence the London fashion scene as the term "New Romantics" was coined – the designer started creating clothes that pointed to the direction for which she would eventually win renown.

McLaren and Westwood stopped working together in 1983 and split up soon after. But Westwood followed her own design trajectory and her 1985 Mini-Crini collection saw the beginning of her trademark corrupted version of Victoriana. Less overtly sexual and more flirtatious, this softening of the harsh fetishism of her punk era remains a staple of Westwood's designs to this day. Always controversial, the fashion designer nevertheless received establishment approval by winning the Womenswear Designer of the Year award in both 1990 and 1991 as well as being given the honour of an OBE for services to fashion in 1992. The last two decades have seen Vivienne Westwood evolve into a millennial mega-brand as well as being the subject of several major retrospective exhibitions paying tribute to a designer who truly changed the face of British fashion.

Kate Moss wearing a red and blue paisley printed crinoline-skirted minidress by Vivienne Westwood, Spring/Summer 1995.

BodyMap

In 1985 BodyMap, the fashion label often associated with the London club scene, was described by the *Chicago Tribune* as "perhaps the hottest, most visually arresting company in Britain's design renaissance." With its trademark prints by textile designer Hilde Smith, cutaway garments and body-altering fabrics, including viscose Lycra, nothing like it had been seen before.

BodyMap was founded in 1982 by fashion graduates Stevie Stewart and David Holah. Respected as stylists as much as fashion designers, the pair created clothes made from fabrics such as jersey, cotton towelling and neoprene, and the way in which they applied these to the human body was genius. These body-con garments were then shrouded in oversized, sculptural layers. Dance-style accessories such as leg warmers completed the look.

Both expert pattern-cutters, Stewart and Holah created garments that overlapped and skimmed the body, a silhouette that gave the impression of shapes that were not really there. They famously didn't discriminate against body shapes, their stretch clothing accommodating all, and happily blurred genders. Their catwalk shows were a form of graphic theatre that throbbed with pop music as Boy George and Marilyn took front-row seats to watch androgynous models free of make-up and dressed in skirts and bra-tops. As Stewart commented to the *Washington Post* in 1984: "We didn't have enough women models, so we put the skirts on men. It looked so well that we decided to show it that way on the catwalk."

BodyMap offered freedom and subtle eroticism. The label folded in the early 1990s, but Stewart and Holah continued to design costumes for artists including Kylie Minogue and Britney Spears, and vintage BodyMap is highly sought after.

Stevie Stewart and David Holah pictured in New York in 1987
wearing some of their more eccentric designs.

Katharine Hamnett

The original fashion activist, Katharine Hamnett became famous for her oversized political slogan T-shirts. Her first design, launched in 1983 and worn by stars including Wham's George Michael, featured the words "CHOOSE LIFE", but it was the controversial shot of Hamnett meeting Prime Minister Margaret Thatcher in 1984 wearing an anti-nuclear war T-shirt with the words "58% DON'T WANT PERSHING" that sealed her reputation as an anti-establishment figure.

> **"The price of clothes may be low, but they are paid for with human lives."**
> *Katharine Hamnett*

Despite commercial and critical success, Hamnett has focused her career on campaigning, not only for political change but for sustainability in fashion, and was an early adopter of organic cotton. In a 2020 interview with the BBC the designer told of her shock and subsequent guilt when in 1989 she started to research fashion's impact on the planet: "The results were devastating, a tsunami of nightmare," she recalled. "Every single material and process had a negative impact – manmade fibres, leather tanning, viscose, dyeing and finishing."

Needless to say, Hamnett's concerns were prescient and today, having relaunched her label in 2017, the designer continues to vigorously campaign for climate action and better ethical standards for both labour and production within the fashion industry.

One of the most famous of Hamnett's designs is the anti-nuclear war T-shirt worn by the designer to meet prime minister Margaret Thatcher in 1984.

Fashion Designers

Margaret Howell

The publicity-shy British designer Margaret Howell exemplifies the unisex approach to fashion that became popular during the late 1970s and 1980s. A long-time admirer of the androgynous, tailored look of icons like Katharine Hepburn, the opening of her first London shop in 1977 serendipitously coincided with the release of the film *Annie Hall*. Women flocked to buy clothes that gave them the effortless cool of Diane Keaton in the movie and Howell's signature look was born.

Taking inspiration from the traditional clothes of her male ancestors – a beloved mackintosh or a well-worn tweed or corduroy jacket – practicality and a passion for traditional fabrics informs all of Howell's designs. As she told *Vogue* in an interview in 2021: "It's all pretty androgynous because, in my lifetime, men's clothes have always been more practical than women's."

There is a spareness to Howell's designs which, combined with masterful execution without unnecessary embellishment, makes them clothes for life not just for today. Her seasonal collections are tweaked just slightly so that everything has a timeless feel, which chimes with today's emphasis on sustainability, and her pared-down aesthetic has won her a legion of lifelong fans. As the designer herself explained to *Vogue*: "Clothes have to be fit for purpose and function, they need to last and be ageless – these principles apply to anything that's well designed."

British designer Margaret Howell photographed in her studio in 1991.
Note the bolts of tweed, a traditional fabric commonly used in her heritage designs.

Bruce Oldfield

Bruce Oldfield was brought up in foster care, learning how to sew from his seamstress foster mother, and as a teenager moved into a charity care home. The designer could not have come from more humble beginnings and yet he is best known for dressing royals and celebrities in stunning luxe evening wear.

A very different kind of British designer to the subversive names of the 1970s and 80s, Oldfield nevertheless had a huge impact on the look of the decade, primarily through his couture designs for Princess Diana. He even gained a reputation as the style icon's favourite designer.

At the time of their meeting, Diana was still wearing the traditional high-necked blouses and floral skirts that so characterized her younger years. Oldfield is widely credited for glamorizing the Princess's wardrobe, creating both elegant daywear and figure-hugging, subtly sexy evening gowns that transformed her from a typical Sloane Ranger to a truly modern royal. His most memorable design was perhaps the open-backed silver lamé dress she wore to the premiere of the James Bond film *A View to a Kill* in 1985. His ability to transcend the conservatism exhibited by many traditional designers of the time had a huge effect on British fashion.

Still working today, Oldfield has dressed a wide range of stylish women over the decades, from Charlotte Rampling and Helen Mirren to Rihanna and Kim Kardashian.

Bruce Oldfield has been widely credited with glamorizing the wardrobe of Princess Diana during the 1980s. One of his most famous designs was the silver lamé gown that she wore to the premiere of the James Bond film *A View to Kill* in 1985.

Fashion Designers

EXTRAVAGANT LUXE

John Galliano

John Galliano is one of Britain's most controversial designers, yet he is widely regarded as a creative genius within his field. Born in 1960 in Gibraltar, he moved to south London with his Spanish mother and Gibraltarian father when he was six years old. Galliano has often attributed his own flamboyance to being raised by his flamenco-dancer mother.

A graduate of Central Saint Martins during a time when the New Romantic fashion subculture was thriving in London, Galliano spent his college years working as a dresser for London's National Theatre, an experience reflected in the theatricality of his subsequent catwalk shows. As fashion historian Kerry Taylor describes it: "Not only were his designs a product of extraordinary feats of imagination and insane workmanship, but also Galliano was one of the first to present each collection as spectacle, a theatrical, immersive experience."

Galliano also took classes studying eighteenth-century clothes construction at the Victoria and Albert Museum, learning skills that would enhance his talent for haute couture as well as feed his lifelong obsession with the grandeur of historical dress. His graduate collection in 1984, titled Les Incroyables, inspired by the drama of the French Revolution,

This shot from 1987 draws heavily on Galliano's favourite theme
of Marie Antoinette. The tongue-in-cheek brooches spelling
"Love To" and "Eat Cake" are a typically playful touch.

This wide-shouldered tailcoat and striped moiré waistcoat paired
with dhoti-style trousers is from Galliano's first major show in
1985, entitled Afghanistan Repudiates Western Ideals.

was bought by fashion boutique Browns. Within a year he had financial backing to start his own label and had befriended his long-time collaborator Amanda Harlech, then a fashion editor for *Harpers & Queen.*

Regrettably, running a business was not Galliano's strong point and by the early 1990s, after his fledgling label went bankrupt, the designer decided to relocate to Paris, where he was known, along with Alexander McQueen, as one of the bad boys of British fashion. Galliano headed up two iconic French fashion houses, Givenchy and then Dior, from where he was famously fired in 2011 after repeated drunken behaviour that culminated in an anti-Semitic outburst. As Dior owned over 90 per cent of Galliano's own label too, he crashed unceremoniously out of the fashion world. It was four years before he returned, as creative director for Maison Martin Margiela in London.

At Dior, his obsession with the exaggerated female form, and his masterful skill in creating architecturally structured clothes, echoed that of the legendary designer himself. Today, at Martin Margiela, Galliano's talent for reinvention has seen him interpret the famously reclusive designer's aesthetic for a changing fashion landscape. Galliano has also designed many memorable and sometimes controversial dresses for famous women, such as the revealing slip-like dark blue Dior dress that Princess Diana wore to the 1996 Met Gala in New York.

John Galliano is undoubtedly one of Britain's greatest couturiers, and his inexhaustible passion for creating clothes is the essence of what makes him such a brilliant designer. As he told *Vogue* in an interview celebrating his 60th birthday in 2020: "Coming back to fashion, I had a longing to focus on the craft above all: that pure creation."

Fashion Designers

Galliano was a favourite designer of the Princess of Wales,
who wore a controversially slinky blue slip dress by the
designer for Dior to the 1996 Met Gala in New York.

Opposite: Galliano has always embraced the theatrical, both in his
designs and his staging. This outfit worn by Helena Christensen for his
Spring/Summer 1997 show has an element of the showgirl about it.

Alexander McQueen

Alexander McQueen was one of the most important fashion designers of his generation. The London-born designer, known as Lee by his friends, left school aged 16 to take up a tailoring apprenticeship on London's historic Savile Row. He subsequently worked for the costumiers Angels and Bermans, an experience that was reflected in his flamboyantly theatrical designs and shows.

This rigorous early training in pattern cutting and gentlemen's tailoring gave McQueen many of the technical skills that so characterized his later designs. In his early 20s McQueen enrolled on the Fashion Design MA at Central Saint Martins. There he immersed himself in not only the course, but in London's abundance of museums and art galleries, both historical and those showing young British artists such as Damien Hirst and Tracey Emin. These years of study, both formal and informal, gave McQueen a rich seam of inspiration on which he drew later in his career.

McQueen's graduate collection, with the macabre title of Jack The Ripper Stalks His Victims, was a remarkable achievement. Inspired by the Whitechapel murders of 1888, the designs, full of technical brilliance, drew on the fashions of the time. Frock coats and ruffled Victorian gowns were printed with butterflies or, more darkly, thorns. The extremes to which McQueen was drawn in his provocative designs were also evident when, in reference to Victorian prostitutes selling their hair, the designer cut off some of his own hair, encased it in silk or Perspex, and sewed it into the linings and labels of his garments.

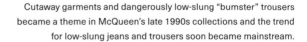
Cutaway garments and dangerously low-slung "bumster" trousers became a theme in McQueen's late 1990s collections and the trend for low-slung jeans and trousers soon became mainstream.

Fashion Designers

McQueen's 1992 collection so impressed legendary stylist Isabella Blow that she bought it in its entirety and in doing so formed a lifelong partnership with the *enfant terrible* of British fashion. During the 1990s, McQueen returned time and time again to Victorian Gothic themes, drawing deeply on the historical archives of the Victoria & Albert Museum, which, he said, "never fail to intrigue and inspire me."

McQueen's first solo collection, entitled Taxi Driver, was a very different production from his later shows, which were operatic in scale and drama, but it did offer a glimpse of one of the 1990s most famous fashion trends: the bumster trouser. Although it wasn't until 1996 that McQueen properly launched the bumster on the catwalk, he made a pair in 1992 for Trixie Bellair, his drag artist friend. For McQueen, the exaggeratedly low-cut trousers, with their revealing bum cleavage, offered not only the power to shock, but unrivalled eroticism. As he told the *Guardian* in 2009: "To me, that part of the body – not so much the buttocks but the bottom of the spine – that's the most erotic part of anyone's body, man or woman."

The contrast between the McQueen's exquisitely tailored trousers and the slightly tasteless flesh reveal summed up much of what the designer aimed to do with his clothes: impress and slightly shock.

During the 1990s, McQueen's collections made political as well as aesthetic statements – for example, his Autumn/Winter 1995 show, Highland Rape, referenced England's violation of Scotland. His theatrical presentations grew ever-more wild: McQueen's 1997 show, renamed Untitled after backers baulked at the name Golden Shower, saw

This stunning voluminous high-necked red silk taffeta gown, designed by Sarah Burton for Alexander McQueen in 2019, harks back to the legendary British designer's love of the baroque.

Fashion Designers

During the finale of McQueen's Spring/Summer 1999 show Shalom Harlow's dress was famously spray-painted by robots.

models drenched in golden-hued water from a sprinkler. A year later, a model was circled by a ring of fire to fit the Joan of Arc theme and most famous of all was the finale to his Spring/Summer 1999 show when Shalom Harlow's dress was spray-painted by robots. In keeping with his fascination with the Brit Art scene, McQueen was not afraid of courting controversy, such as with trapped models appearing in a glass box for his Spring/Summer 2001 show, Voss. Nevertheless,

the designer received the accolade of British Designer of the Year four times during his career.

Like Galliano, McQueen was courted by the French fashion houses, heading up Givenchy from 1996 to 2001 before returning to London to focus on his eponymous label. The next decade, before he tragically took his own life in 2010, saw McQueen go from strength to strength both artistically and commercially. A truly unique talent, Alexander McQueen has gone down in fashion history and his name continues to be one of the most important in the fashion world.

McQueen's shows and designs became increasingly complex and aesthetically challenging as his career progressed. In this outfit from his Autumn/Winter 2009 show a model swathed in feathers appears trapped, her wings folded.

Never afraid of controversy, McQueen's 1997 show was presented as Untitled after his backers, American Express, reputedly baulked at the name Golden Shower.

Birds and feathers, complete with a Hitchcock-like terror
of attack, are a recurring theme in McQueen's outfits and
staging since his 1995 show entitled The Birds.

The intricacy of McQueen's designs is illustrated here in this
chiffon dress, heavily embroidered with lace. The matching veil and
antlers headdress is a classic combination of the designer.

Hussein Chalayan

The same year that Alexander McQueen completed his MA at Central Saint Martins, Hussein Chalayan graduated from the BA Fashion Design course. Speaking at the Victoria and Albert Museum in 2011, the Cypriot-born British designer described the college's uniquely rich creative environment: "The differences in students created a really diverse environment and fellow students' comments about each other's work sometimes mattered more than some of the tutors."

Always experimental, Chalayan's final show featured silk dresses that he had buried and then dug up from his garden. Like many other promising young British designers, his entire collection was bought by fashion boutique Browns.

The avant-garde designer is best known for his uniquely innovative approach to fashion, in which he combines disciplines including architecture, sculpture and installation art. Some of his most memorable designs include coffee tables that metamorphose into skirts, gowns with airplane wings and an origami-style dress that folds into an envelope. Seen as an intellectual, Chalayan has struggled to succeed commercially despite his remarkable creations. Nevertheless, he has made an important contribution to the London fashion scene, his limitless imagination characteristic of those who have broken boundaries in British fashion since the 1960s. He received an OBE in 2006 and was made an honorary fellow of the London College of Fashion in 2011.

Fashion Designers

Chalayan's infamous coffee table skirt. His skill with sculptural designs that verge on installation art have given the experimental designer his reputation as the intellectual of the fashion world.

Julien Macdonald

Julien Macdonald is best known for his transformation of women's knitwear from something homely and conservative into glamorous, spangled creations, beloved by celebrities and made accessible to ordinary women through his diffusion lines.

The Welsh-born designer trained in fashion knitwear before studying for an MA at the Royal College of Art. On his graduation in 1996, Macdonald was appointed Head of Knitwear Design for Chanel and also Karl Lagerfeld's own label, after the legendary German designer was impressed by his final collection. One example, now held by the Victoria & Albert Museum, is a 1930s inspired evening dress intricately knitted from viscose and lurex, which took Macdonald three weeks to make.

Macdonald worked for Lagerfeld for two years before succeeding Alexander McQueen at Givenchy in 2001, a post he remained in until 2004 before returning to London to concentrate on his own designs.

The perfect ambassador for the luxe glamour of the 1990s and early 2000s, Macdonald has created dresses for stars including Kylie Minogue, Gwyneth Paltrow and also Beyoncé, a long-time client of the designer. As the designer told *Style of the City* magazine in 2018: "My clothes really empower a woman, making her feel glamorous, special and like a superstar."

Fashion Designers

Beloved of many celebrities, Macdonald has also created numerous stage costumes for artists including Beyoncé, pictured here performing in Los Angeles in 2016.

2000s – present day:

FASHION FOR A NEW MILLENIUM

Stella McCartney

Daughter of former Beatle Paul McCartney and photographer and animal rights activist Linda McCartney, Stella McCartney has transcended her parent's fame to become one of Britain's foremost fashion designers.

McCartney, who started making her own clothes aged 13, showed a commitment to the fashion industry early on, taking up a youthful internship with Christian Lacroix and spending a period with Savile Row tailor Edward Sexton. A graduate of Central Saint Martins in 1995, the designer left in a cloud of notoriety when models Kate Moss and Naomi Campbell famously walked in her degree show, something she admits she now regrets, telling Radio 4's *Desert Island Discs*: "I look back on that moment and just feel a bit embarrassed that I was so naïve."

McCartney immediately set up her own label and, more than two decades later, has long since silenced any early critics, becoming a leading player in the fashion world. Aged just 25, McCartney took over from Karl Lagerfeld as creative director of Chloé in 1997 but, her heart in London, returned to her own label in 2001. Devoted to animal welfare, sustainability and ethical practices, she continues to design her signature

Fashion Designers

Naomi Campbell walking the catwalk in an outfit for Stella
McCartney's graduation in 1995. The designer notoriously called
upon her famous supermodel friends to appear in the show.

style of relaxed luxe tailoring. In an interview with *Women's Wear Daily* McCartney explained: "It's not about what it looks like in the studio or on the runway, it's what it looks like on a real person that matters."

Perhaps the most important contributions McCartney has made to the world of fashion design is her commitment to animal rights, reflected within her own collections by her refusal to use animal products, and her campaign for a more sustainable fashion industry. As she told the *Financial Times* in 2021: "I just want to help save the planet." As the designer of the world's first vegan "It" bag, McCartney displayed great moral resolve, especially in the early days of her career, in rejecting the use of any leather, fur, feathers or other animal skin. Her company has long pioneered the use of alternative materials that she has designed in such a way to match the luxury of animal products, and more recent innovations include spider silk and mycelium leather.

With today's increased awareness of climate change and planetary destruction, she continues to strive toward using oil-free and completely plant-based products as well as reworking second-hand clothes and fabrics. She is currently working with LVMH advising on sustainability and, despite daily news of the depletion of the planet, remains optimistic that things can change, telling fashionista.com: "You've got to give people solutions, and you've got to encourage them with some level of hope."

Fashion Designers

As a long-time ardent animal rights campaigner, McCartney has long pioneered the use of alternative materials. Her fake fur and leather-free vegan footwear and accessories have become increasingly sought after.

Burberry

Thomas Burberry founded the quintessential British fashion house in 1856, and in 1879 made his name as the inventor of gabardine, the ground-breaking waterproof fabric that was both light and durable. The iconic Burberry trench coat was born, although it was not until the 1920s that its signature checked "Nova" lining appeared. Gaining a royal warrant in 1955 and silver-screen fame when worn by actors including Audrey Hepburn, Marlene Dietrich and Humphrey Bogart, Burberry seemed firmly established amongst the world's social elite.

By the 1990s, however, a different story was emerging. Burberry's profits were poor and to add to this, troubled British soap star actress Danniella Westbrook was photographed in 2002 dressed head to toe in Burberry check, accessorized by baby and pram in the same print. It seemed the brand's reputation might never recover after luxury London department stores such as Selfridges and Harvey Nichols dropped the label overnight.

Fortunately, British fashion designer Christopher Bailey, who joined Burberry in 2001, turned its fortunes around. Bringing its catwalk shows back to London in 2009, launching the philanthropic Burberry foundation, and a careful advertising campaign featuring British stars such as Kate Moss and Eddie Redmayne were moves that once again sealed Burberry's reputation as one of Britain's oldest, and most successful, fashion houses. Riccardo Tisci took over as Chief Creative Officer in 2018, and the luxury brand continues to thrive.

Fashion Designers

Over recent years Burberry's fortunes have once again revived and the iconic Nova heritage check, shown here on the catwalk in 2020, goes from strength to strength.

Christopher Kane

Glasgow-born fashion designer Christopher Kane is another alumnus of Central Saint Martins, one whose experimental approach to fashion has made him one the most innovative designers of his generation. His 2006 final collection, full of stretch lace dresses and brass-chain accessories, not only won Kane the Harrods Design Award, it so impressed Donatella Versace that the Italian fashion maven offered him a consultancy role.

On setting up his own label after graduation, Kane quickly established his signature style of sexy, bondage-tight designs made from neon elastics in a range of bright blues, pinks and purples. Gradually softening his body-con look to develop a more relaxed silhouette, Kane is notable for using luxe fabrics including leather, velvet, snakeskin and chiffon, often creatively juxtaposed with more unusual textures such as plastic and crochet.

As a bold new British designer Kane was the perfect fit for a collaboration with London store Topshop, the prime destination for young fashion lovers. His own brand started with a capsule collection in 2007, later expanding to cover women's ready-to-wear as well as accessories including bags and shoes. Kane has also had successful long-time collaborations with notable names including crystal-makers Swarovski and legendary shoe designer Manolo Blahnik.

In 2009 Kane launched a line of T-shirts featuring his trademark monkey print and his appeal was such that his Spring/Summer 2009 collection, launched on elite fashion site Net-a-Porter, completely sold out within 24 hours. Over the last decade Kane has gone from strength to strength, forming a temporary partnership with luxury goods conglomerate Kering before taking back full control of his eponymous brand in 2018.

One of Kane's early collections of typically bright
bondage-style dresses from Spring/Summer 2007.

Pugh has been unafraid to push the boundaries of fashion from the very beginning of his career as illustrated by the masked model wearing a structural black and white harlequin costume from his groundbreaking Spring/Summer 2007 show.

Gareth Pugh

Avant-garde British designer Gareth Pugh originally trained as a dancer and also worked in the costume department of the National Youth Theatre, both experiences which informed his later work.

Born in the north-east of England, Pugh has always been fascinated by the mix of sleaze and glamour in London, often standing side by side. While he was at Central Saint Martins, his aesthetic became increasingly dark and his final show saw red and white balloons tied to models' various body parts, a shocking yet mesmerizing presentation that subsequently appeared on the cover of *Dazed* magazine.

From the start, Pugh has pushed fashion to extremes. His first, groundbreaking Spring/Summer 2007 show featured masked models in oversized, structural black and white harlequin costumes, the inclusion of sensual latex giving the collection a nightclub vibe. The slightly sinister subtext of his designs, often harking back to the Victorian Gothic or Elizabethan eras, are characteristic of Pugh's fashion to this day.

Pugh has further experimented by presenting his collections through media other than the catwalk, especially dance and film. The three films he has collaborated on with filmmaker Ruth Hogben create visually disturbing narratives: one features a model cutting her hair before smearing herself with blood-like red paint in the shape of the St George's flag.

Featured by the Victoria and Albert Museum and the Costume Institute at the Metropolitan Museum of Art, Pugh's work often seems to extend from mere fashion into the worlds of sculpture and installation art. Ever fascinated by theatre and dance, the designer has created costumes for artists including Beth Ditto.

Fashion Designers

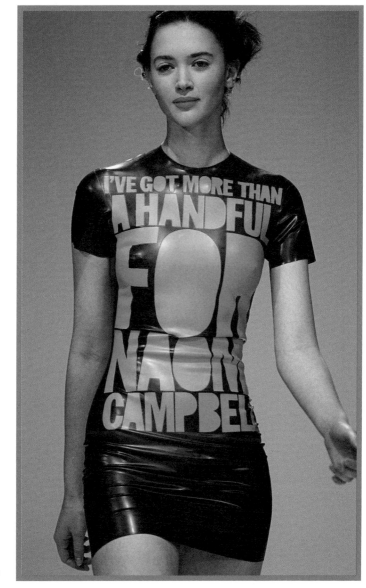

Henry Holland

Manchester-born Henry Holland, who initially worked as a fashion editor for teen magazines, burst onto the fashion scene in 2006 when fellow designer Gareth Pugh walked out onto the catwalk at the end of his show wearing a T-shirt with the words, "Get Yer Freak On Giles Deacon", in homage to his contemporary.

The words, one of several rhyming slogans, were the tongue-in-cheek creation of Henry Holland, and suddenly they were the hottest thing in fashion. Other irreverent designs that appeared proudly emblazoned across the chests of the fashion crowd included, "Let's play naked Twister Linda Evangelista", "I'll Tell You Who's Boss Kate Moss", and "Let's breed Bella Hadid".

As Holland admitted in an interview with the *Guardian* in 2009: "Yeah, I started my entire business as a joke, which sounds bad, doesn't it?" Nevertheless, off the back of his T-shirts the House of Holland was born, injecting some much-needed quirkiness into the British fashion scene. Over the last 15 years Henry Holland has collaborated with many other brands to bring his signature bright colours, prints and playful style to the masses.

Unfortunately, like so many others in the fashion world, House of Holland went into administration in 2020 during the Covid-19 pandemic. However, Holland himself remains optimistic for the future, telling *Vogue* at the time: "I will never enter a job that doesn't fill me with endless joy and pride. For that I will always have House of Holland to thank."

Model wearing one of Henry Holland's irreverent logo T-shirts for the Autumn/Winter 2007 House of Holland show.

Fashion Designers

Ashish

Indian-born designer Ashish Gupta is part of a new generation of London designers that continue to make the city one of the most exciting in the fashion world. An homage to his Indian heritage, Gupta's signature is the use of sequins, once associated with cheap market clothing but transformed by the designer's unique vision into kaleidoscopic creations in kaleidoscopic colours.

Since 2005, the label Ashish has juxtaposed street style with glamour and luxe evening wear with ironic designs featuring controversial slogans such as "Good Mourning" and a version of the Mastercard logo reading "Masturbate". Gupta's clothes combine tradition with contemporary fashion in exciting creations, such as hybrids of saris and jeans.

The level of diversity in his collections, including gender-fluidity, is inspiring. As he told *Vogue*: "I always want my shows to be a celebration of subcultures."

But his collections are also simply an exhilarating riot of Technicolor outfits, with not only sequins but tinsel, lurex and tulle exploding onto the catwalk in patterns as varied as florals, stars and the designer's own doodles. Unsurprisingly Ashish's designs are sought after by celebrities including Beyoncé, Rita Ora, Jennifer Lopez and Madonna. He follows in the tradition of London designers since the 1960s: nothing is too much.

A model walks the Ashish catwalk in February 2020 wearing a colourful sequinned tribute to major league baseball teams.

Duro Olowu

Nigerian-born, London-based designer Duro Olowu is another contemporary name who blends heritage with the contemporary to create clothes that were described by *Vogue* in 2021 as "a glorious acid trip of swirling print and color".

Citing designers including Issey Miyake, Azzedine Alaïa and Yves Saint Laurent as his inspiration growing up, Olowu draws on varied elements of culture and style in his collections to create beautiful and unique clothes that are, nevertheless, easy to wear. In an interview with writer Alain Elkann in 2017, the designer explained: "The things that inspire me are women, past and present, how they live, see things, what they need. I want to make women feel confident in an effortless way."

It was in 2004 that Olowu shot to fame with his "Duro" dress, a bohemian, empire-waisted, kimono-like gown with wide, graceful sleeves, made from a patchwork of his own prints and remnants of vintage couture fabrics. His goal in creating the dress was to make women feel "free, chic and full of joie de vivre."

Although Olowu now only designs for special orders, his collections over the past two decades have continued to remain true to his early vision. His knowledge and interest in art, especially early and contemporary African art and Surrealism, has informed his designs, which feature bold prints and are pleasingly structural in design. His creations, which appear regularly on the red carpet, are beloved of a number of celebrities including Michelle Obama, Saoirse Ronan, Thandiwe Newton and Jane Levy.

Detail from a 2010 outfit by Duro Olowu, showing the intricate craftsmanship and use of colour in his work.

Fashion Designers

Daniel Lee

Rising British fashion star Daniel Lee, who worked at Maison Margiela and Balenciaga before spending six years working alongside Phoebe Philo at Céline, is tipped to be one of the biggest names in the business thanks to his revival of the Italian fashion brand Bottega Veneta. Lee took over as creative director in 2018, transforming the label from staid classic to luxe streetwear in just three years before announcing his departure in 2021, and winning four awards at the British Fashion Awards.

With his finger firmly on the pulse of street style, Lee created textural designs for Bottega Veneta which brought the label to a new millennial and Gen Z consumer. The modernizing of the brand's signature *intrecciato* woven leather by supersizing bags in his trademark "parakeet" green, along with the creation of a new icon, the cassette bag, complete with chunky gold chain, and "puddle" boots, made from rubber, have made Lee popular among celebrities of the likes of Stormzy, Kanye West and Mary J. Blige.

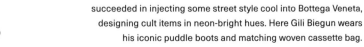

During his short tenure at the classic fashion house, Daniel Lee succeeded in injecting some street style cool into Bottega Veneta, designing cult items in neon-bright hues. Here Gili Biegun wears his iconic puddle boots and matching woven cassette bag.

Christopher Raeburn

Since 2006, Christopher Raeburn has made his name as a pioneer in sustainable fashion. His clothes, made from repurposed fabrics as varied as military parachutes, life rafts and other remnants that would otherwise go to waste, have become increasingly sought after as the fashion industry wakes up to its impact on the planet.

His company, RÆBURN, has worked for over a decade to increase awareness of sustainability issues within the fashion industry. Initiatives include the East London Studio where old clothes are remade into contemporary fashion, an Asia-based recycling programme, and a focus on waste reduction and local manufacturing. Though his is a relatively niche brand with a high price point, Raeburn's message is important in a world where greenwashing and shouting about eco credentials is part of many mainstream brands' strategies.

As he told highsnobiety.com in 2021: "A lot of the work that's happened in the last five years, particularly around recycled materials and circularity...all of this gives me a lot of hope that the foundations are there for a much more positive future."

With sustainability such an important issue in the fashion world, there are a number of other young British designers following in Raeburn's footsteps. These include the menswear designer Bethany Williams; Priya Ahluwalia, who uses textile techniques to rejuvenate secondhand and deadstock clothing; and Patrick McDowell, who works with brands including Burberry and Swarovski to promote circularity and reduce fashion's global impact.

A model walks the catwalk in 2018 wearing a coat and carrying a bag from Raeburn's sustainable collection.

Fashion Designers

chapter 3

STYLE iCONS

1960S/70S

The Swinging Sixties saw a transformation in London's fashion scene, with teenagers, secretaries, celebrities and socialites all embracing the same trends. Restaurants such as Alexander's in the basement of Mary Quant's shop Bazaar proved popular meeting places, and shoppers at venerated store Biba rubbed shoulders with the style elite.

Style icons of Swinging London included gamine models – the ultra-lean Twiggy, Jean Shrimpton and Pattie Boyd – all of whom suited the bold, miniskirted fashion of the decade. Boyd married George Harrison in 1966, and the Beatles themselves also influenced fashion, racing through trends at top speed, from matching suits and Beatle boots to the hippy vibe immortalized on Peter Blake's sleeve design for *Sgt. Pepper's Lonely Hearts Club Band*.

The Rolling Stones were also outlandish in their style, especially when it came to playing with gender roles. With his feminine-cut suits, Mick Jagger rivalled David Bowie (himself later a massive influence on androgynous style), and famously took to the stage in 1969 wearing a white dress. Keith Richards had a love of luxe attire and could regularly be seen wearing Persian lambskin coats, snakeskin boots and velvet in dark purple hues. Jagger's girlfriend during the late 1960s, singer-songwriter Marianne Faithfull, was a notable

Style Icons

Super-slim 1960s model Twiggy redefined the beauty of the decade and became a new kind of style icon. Pictured here wearing a bright pink minidress typical of its time.

Sixties rock girlfriends Marianne Faithfull and Anita Pallenberg at Heathrow Airport in 1967 on their way to join their respective partners, both members of the Rolling Stones, Mick Jagger and Keith Richards.

Pop star Sandie Shaw in 1964 wearing her signature look of mod-style cigarette pants and turtleneck, feet bare as always.

style icon too, and her effortlessly cool mix of short suede skirts and mohair sweaters, long fur coats, floppy hat and oversized sunglasses inspires to this day.

Singer Sandie Shaw had a very on-point 1960s look, too, wearing a mix of bohemian dresses and mod-style cigarette pants with turtleneck sweater, set off by her signature bare feet. And Liverpudlian songstress Cilla Black was credited by Biba founder Barbara Hulanicki in her autobiography as

Style Icons

Liverpudlian singer Cilla Black was a big fan of 1960s fashions and a regular at both Mary Quant's shop Bazaar and legendary fashion emporium, Biba. She is pictured here in a classic 1960s printed monochrome minidress.

Pattie Boyd, model and wife of Beatle George Harrison, had an elfin look that epitomized everything about the playful 1960s. In this shot from 1966 she is wearing a Hoopla miniskirt from the London boutique Quorum, for which Ossie Clark and Celia Birtwell designed.

Style Icons

achieving the perfect 1960s image, of "fresh little foals with long legs, bright faces and round dolly eyes." Fashion muse Jane Birkin exported the Swinging London look to Paris, and made it her own.

The 1970s were a decade of outlandish styles, and those who loved fashion hyperbole were in their element. Icons included Elton John with his flamboyant stage costumes, and Rod Stewart, once dubbed "Rod the Mod", in velvet suits or printed blazers, embracing bright colours and metallics that just touched on glam. For the anti-fashion crowd, a very different style to the glamour of stage and screen was found

The Rolling Stones were notable fashion icons during the 1960s and 1970s, both on and off stage. Their favourite off-duty look was a dandyish mix of luxe tailoring and stylized accessories. Pictured here walking in London's Green Park.

in punk, a trend immortalized by the Sex Pistols, who were undeniably style icons in their own, if not perverted, way.

Although not British herself, actress and model Anita Pallenberg certainly qualified as a London style icon during the 1960s and 70s thanks to her status as rock super-groupie and original rock 'n' roll "It" girl. The partner of the Rolling Stones' Keith Richards, Pallenberg had a look that was dubbed "evil glamour" by Marianne Faithfull. From paisley print minidresses, suede jackets and feather boas to silk blouses, kaftans and leopard-print flares, Pallenberg epitomized bohemian rock fashion.

David Bowie was a huge style influencer during the 1970s, pushing gender boundaries and rejecting fashion norms. Pictured here in 1973 onstage in Los Angeles during his Ziggy Stardust era.

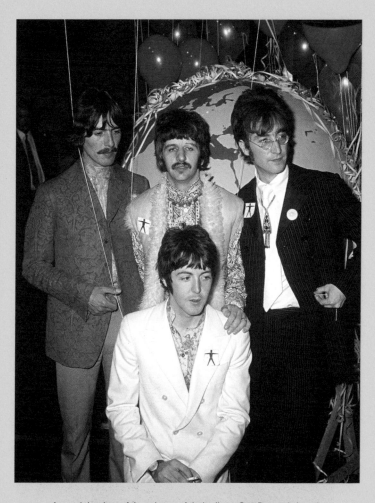

Around the time of the release of their album *Sgt. Pepper's Lonely Hearts Club Band*, the Beatles embraced the multicoloured, richly textural medley that marked the beginning of the hippy era.

English model Jean Shrimpton, pictured in 1964, managed to juxtapose sophistication and youthful style.

1980S

There was a style dichotomy in London in the 1980s between the upper-class Sloane Rangers and their icon, Princess Diana, and the alternative New Romantics, epitomized by the likes of Boy George.

During the 1980s Princess Diana was the most famous woman in the world and much copied. And her confidence in her fashion choices mirrored a growing belief in herself. The early 1980s saw a demure young woman dressed in Laura Ashley floral dresses and skirts, matched with blouses with frill collars or pussy bows and neat cardigans, topped off with that famous flicked hairstyle. By the latter part of the decade the princess was lunching in smart tailored suits and wowing in stunning evening wear, largely thanks to British designer Bruce Oldfield. As the decade drew to a close, Diana became more sophisticated in her style, picking big-name international designers and sparking some truly memorable fashion moments.

A more contemporary-looking 1980s icon was that of one of Britain's most successful female pop artists, Nigerian-born Sade. Unsurprisingly given her polished style, the singer was a graduate of Central Saint Martins and had worked as a fashion designer and model before joining the pop scene in the early 1980s. Her mix of sophisticated monochromes and dress-down denim looks current to this day.

Not everyone was extreme in the 1980s. Singer Kim Wilde sums up what 80s style means to a lot of people in her high-waisted skinny jeans and striped T-shirt, with blazer or biker jacket, stilettos, obligatory overdone makeup and bouffant

Scottish singer Annie Lennox pictured on stage
in 1987 wearing a studded leather suit.

hair topping off the look. Likewise, Annie Lennox flew under
the radar with her understated fashion choices, preferring
oversized, baggy men's suits as a foil to her close-cropped
bleached or coloured hair, a style that has inspired several
more recent fashion designers to revisit the iconic 1980s look.

Style Icons

Princess Diana at Guards Polo Club wearing her signature casual look of faded jeans, oversized tailored jacket, baseball cap and cowboy boots.

This purple evening gown which the princess wore in 1987 sums up 1980s style. Designed by Catherine Walker, it has a velvet bodice and silk taffeta flamenco-style skirt.

This portrait of Boy George from the early 1980s sums up the legendary singer's ability to individualize the fashion of the decade with his own unique flair. He is accompanied by performance artist, fashion designer and style influencer Leigh Bowery.

With her alternative, exaggerated style, Siouxsie Sioux mixed punk with goth-like glamour and a flair for the theatrical both on and off stage. Photographed here in London in 1983.

Style Icons

The original New Romantic band, Spandau Ballet, dressed in outfits which include drape jackets, satin dressing gowns, cutaway Edwardian-style frock coats and leather trousers, accessorized by costume jewellery. Full make-up and copious amounts of hair gel were obligatory.

Style Icons

During the 1980s pop star Sade had a sophisticated style. This backless white top with sleek-fitting black skirt ensemble, which she wore on stage in 1985, still looks remarkably contemporary.

1990S

Post the vibrant yellow smiley faces and shapelessness of acid house rave fashion, style watchers were ripe for a bit of glamour, and it took just one dress to make a new style icon. In 1994 Elizabeth Hurley, a little-known English actress, wore a plunging black Versace dress, split up the side and held together by safety pins, to the premiere of the film *Four Weddings and a Funeral*, changing the way red-carpet style would be seen for ever.

A new London supermodel, Kate Moss, began popularizing a waif-like silhouette that hadn't been seen since the 1960s. Her physique perfectly suited the tiny slip dresses she wore throughout the 90s, more often than not topped by a grungy leather jacket. Fellow Londoner and model Naomi Campbell had a very different style, favouring glamorous dresses, often sheer or slit to the thigh, in bright colours and luxe fabrics, often adorned with sparkle. Both supermodels were closely watched and emulated by young women and have endured as style icons to this day.

The 1990s also produced the Spice Girls, perhaps an unlikely set of style icons but their over-the-top looks, which covered every style base from tracksuits to body-con dresses and animal prints, summed up the (girl) power of making unapologetic fashion choices.

Style Icons

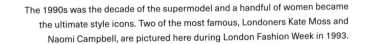

The 1990s was the decade of the supermodel and a handful of women became the ultimate style icons. Two of the most famous, Londoners Kate Moss and Naomi Campbell, are pictured here during London Fashion Week in 1993.

Actress Elizabeth Hurley in the daring safety pin Versace dress that she wore to the premiere of *Four Weddings and a Funeral* in 1994. The revealing dress made headlines and changed the face of acceptable red-carpet fashion.

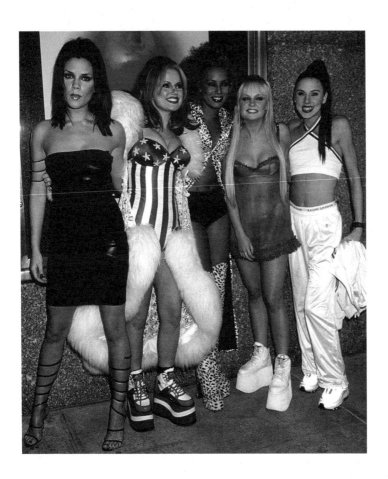

Unlikely style icons, the Spice Girls nevertheless captured the spirit of girl power complete with in-your-face fashion choices during the late 1990s and early 2000s. Shown here at the MTV Music Video Awards in 1997.

Style Icons

Model, DJ and presenter Alexa Chung has become a street style icon for a new generation. Her signature look during London Fashion Week in 2013 is comprised of a black leather miniskirt and simple cream knit.

While many fashion icons of the early 2000s came from America, London has given us plenty of examples of confident women with an innate sense of style. Take Sienna Miller, who was catapulted into the limelight after meeting Jude Law in 2003, and immediately sparked a trend for boho. Her early, artfully dishevelled look, with its Navajo influences, low-slung belts and Western boots, has evolved into smart-casual tailoring as the years have passed, and Miller is as at home on the red carpet as at a festival.

Alexa Chung's style is in the same, effortless mode, making classics such as striped T-shirts and denim shorts, leather skirts, ballet pumps, white shirts and a trench coat look timelessly fashionable, and inspiring thousands of haircuts in an attempt to emulate her artfully dishevelled locks. Victoria Beckham epitomizes another iconic look altogether, that of the polished professional – she is a successful modern woman who owns her glossy style, inspiring many others. Fashion influencers who prefer to stay behind the scenes but nevertheless have a huge impact include the legendary stylist Katie Grand.

Today style icons need to push boundaries further and further – and who better to do that than Harry Styles? The British singer, the first male to appear solo on the cover of *Vogue* magazine (incidentally wearing a dress), has inspired a new generation of style lovers with his rejection of gender distinction and uninhibited willingness to explore every avenue fashion has to offer.

Style Icons

The early 2000s trend for boho was personified by actress Sienna Miller whose love of hippy prints, oversized hats and artful dishevelment sparked a new type of cool. Pictured here with then-boyfriend Jude Law in 2004.

Style Icons

Victoria Beckham has emerged from her days as part of the Spice Girls to become a fashion designer with her own perfectly polished sense of style. Seen here during Paris Fashion week in 2018.

No recent figure has done more to popularize the blurring of gender stereotypes in fashion as Harry Styles, making him one of the most important style icons of his generation. For the 2019 Met Gala the singer confidently mixed tuxedo trousers with a semi-sheer lace blouse and his trademark pearl earring.

chapter 4

STREET STYLE

TEDDY BOYS

"Street style" emerged as an umbrella term in fashion after the Second World War, coinciding with the arrival of various subcultures. Wearing the styles associated with these alternative movements was a way for young people to identify with a certain tribe. London was a particularly ripe environment for fashion subcultures from the 1950s onwards.

Teddy boys were the first fashion subculture to strut London's streets. They were a group of predominantly working-class, disconsolate young men who had latched on to dance, jazz and later rock 'n' roll as a fundamental part of their culture.

The Teds, as they preferred to be known, were first labelled "Teddy boy" in 1953 in the *Daily Express,* after the adapted Edwardian Romanticism they liked to wear. This London version of the American zoot suit was characterized by tailored, velvet-collared draped jackets, drainpipe trousers, skinny ties and crepe-soled brothel-creeper shoes, topped off by a greased quiff hairstyle.

Ironically, in the early 1950s, traditional Savile Row tailors had been pushing a post-war revival of flamboyant Edwardian fashions as a reaction to wartime austerity. However, as reported in the *Londonderry Sentinel* in September 1954, in an article titled "The Style the 'Teddy Boys' Killed", the associations with violence quickly made this the fashion of rebellious teenagers.

Street Style

A group of Teddy Boys pose on a London street corner in 1955. The tailored three-piece suits, skinny tie and velvet collared jacket are typical of the look.

MODS VERSUS ROCKERS

Bitter rivals who clashed in riots on the British beaches during the holiday weekends of 1964, the mods and rockers were the two most famous subcultures of the 1960s.

The mods were initially considered the respectable face of British youth, in part thanks to their smart appearance. As the first generation of teens not bound by National Service, and young enough not to remember wartime austerity, their "modern" lifestyle was one of music, fine clothes and easy spending. Drugs were rife, as was partying, but immaculate styling was the most important part of the movement. It was this obsession with dress, along with a degree of snobbishness, that so offended the rockers.

Considered an offshoot of the Teddy boys, mods favoured a slim tailored Italian-style three-piece suit, always with a narrow lapel and often checked, along with brogues or winkle-picker shoes. When on their trusty Vespa or Lambretta scooter, this outfit was topped with their signature military-green fishtail hooded parka coat, worn to protect their expensive outfits. Female mods were sometimes androgynous, wearing similar tailored trousers to their male counterparts, or if they were fashion-aware they looked to Mary Quant's styles, including the shortest of miniskirts and bold monochrome prints.

In contrast, rockers, taking their lead from the United States' rock 'n' roll scene, wore patched and studded biker leathers and scruffy denims, with white socks rolled over their boots. Their hair was heavily lacquered in a pompadour style.

Street Style

A group of leather-clad Rockers pictured with their motorbikes
on London's Embankment during the 1960s.

A group of Mods in their instantly recognizable fishtail parkas, worn to protect
their smart suits, ride their scooters along the Hastings seafront in 1964.

Street Style

A pair of dancers, cigarettes hanging from their mouths, do the Milk the Cow dance at London's Flamingo club in 1964.

A lone dancer keeps going when, on 5 December 1965, garage pop band The Cardinals attempted to beat the 102 hours continuous playing record at London's The New Scene club.

Street Style

These rebels without a cause rode motorbikes, listened to Elvis Presley and considered Marlon Brando their style icon. Unlike the mods, who were seen as part of the dandified 1960s fashion revolution, the rockers still had their feet firmly in the macho 1950s.

HIPPIES

The freedom-loving, flower-power counterculture of the late 1960s into the 1970s was a crucial subculture in Britain. Their laid-back attitudes were strongly associated with a particular kind of music, and hippy tunes were fostered by pirate radio stations, particularly John Peel and his show, The Perfumed Garden, on Radio London. Hits like the Beatles' *Sgt. Pepper's Lonely Hearts Club Band* epitomized the hippy spirit and took it to a wider audience.

Festivals played a big part, too, and while the US is famous for Woodstock in 1969, the same year saw 150,000 fans visit the Isle of Wight to hear Bob Dylan and the Who play live, and Glastonbury was held for the first time in September 1970.

Fashion is perhaps the most recognizable thing about the hippy movement. The loose silhouette featuring free-flowing long peasant skirts and kaftans meant liberation for women, literally and symbolically. As anti-capitalists and dislikers of rules in general, hippies rejected outright any sartorial diktats of the previous two decades. There was also a strong ecological and environmental thrust to the movement, meaning that clothes and other fabrics were recycled. London's wealth of secondhand shops proved rich hunting ground as vintage garments were adopted and reworked, and textures and patterns were piled one on top of another.

Although hippies gave way to the edgier punks towards the end of the 1970s, their style remains a recurring influence in fashion to this day.

Street Style

A group of hippies at Bardney Pop Festival in 1972. The jeans, floral jackets, wide brimmed hats and unkempt long hair are typical of the hippy look.

Overleaf: *A Saturday Morning 3,* colour lithograph by Malcolm English from *Carnaby Street* (1970) by Tom Salter, owner of the street's influential store Gear.

PUNK

It is impossible to talk about punk without crediting fashion icon Vivienne Westwood, her then partner Malcolm McLaren, and the Sex Pistols, the band that became the face of punk rock. The pair's King's Road shop was renamed Too Young to Live, Too Fast to Die in 1972, a tribute to James Dean and the teenage disillusionment he represented, and it was here that punk fashion arrived.

As with other subcultures, anti-establishment viewpoints were at the heart of punk, but they had no fixed place on the political spectrum. Left-wing punks were against the military, defenders of individualism and pro racial equality, but their right-wing counterparts identified with beliefs as extreme as neo-Nazism. Many punks simply adopted the most offensive

These punks in broken-down denim, metal-studded belts and hard rock T-shirts also sport the signature gelled spiked hairstyle which became popular during the 1970s.

Street Style

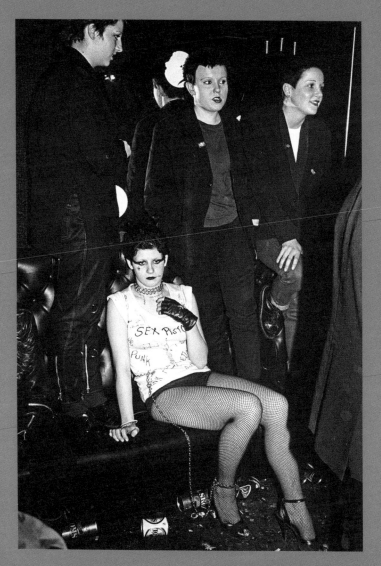

Punks at London's Roxy club in 1977. The DIY Sex Pistols T-shirt and fishnets exemplify the self-customized nature of punk fashion.

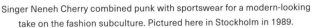

Singer Neneh Cherry combined punk with sportswear for a modern-looking take on the fashion subculture. Pictured here in Stockholm in 1989.

symbols they could find, just to shock. What did unify the punk movement, however, was their fashion sense.

Westwood's unique brand of fashion deconstructionism was perfect for the destructive momentum behind punk. Clothes were ripped and torn, leather jackets were sprayed with painted slogans or motifs and embellished with metal studs and pins. Jewellery meant thick neck chains and multiple piercings, and hair was aggressively gelled and spiked. Westwood's notorious T-shirts featured irreverent and disturbing images such as Mickey Mouse having sex, cowboys showing their genitals and the Queen with a safety pin through her lip.

As the 1970s progressed, London's disconsolate youth flocked to the King's Road shop, now named Seditionaries, to confirm punk's status as the home of anarchic rebels, and the subculture spread out across the UK. One particular outfit now held by the Victoria and Albert Museum was made from old army-surplus gear; a netted red and white scarf, looking much as if it had been blood soaked, was draped militia style across the chest. The punks were going to war.

Although Westwood began to move towards New Romanticism by the end of the decade, punk persisted through the 1980s and beyond. Piercings and tattoos were the signature of 1980s punks but clothing had become more diverse, although slogan T-shirts, metal-studded leather, distressed denim and heavy boots were still part of the look. It was the brightly dyed Mohican or spiked hairstyles that really defined the 1980s punk, along with the obligatory hard stare and fighting attitude.

The 1990s saw much of punk music soften but, ironically given its anti-materialistic origins, since the turn of the millennium this style subculture has been adopted by mainstream fashion.

NEW ROMANTiCS

In 1981, disillusioned with the direction in which punk was moving, Vivienne Westwood sparked the next major trend – the New Romantics. According to the V&A, the clothes, showcased in a collection titled Pirate, evoked an "age of highwaymen, dandies and buccaneers".

Inspired by Westwood's love of seventeenth- and eighteenth-century portrait paintings, and promoted by her partner Malcolm McLaren's band Bow Wow Wow, the New Romantic look was quickly adopted by the music and club scenes. Steve Strange's Blitz night in Covent Garden popularized the fashion which was embraced by artists including Spandau Ballet and Culture Club.

Drawing on influences as varied as Russian constructivism, Bonnie Prince Charlie, 1930s cabaret, and the Pierrot clown, the main components of the New Romantic look were historical eccentricity, gender-fluidity and extravagance.

The press weren't sure what to make of this new aesthetic, flamboyant in its use of full make-up, larger-than-life hair and luxe fabrics. As Dylan Jones, author of the book *Sweet Dreams: The Story of the New Romantics*, writes, they were condemned as "effete show-offs who were playing dress-up, but actually they all came from North London council estates."

The trend burned bright but fast and by 1985 was on its way out. One of the last designers to express its influence was John Galliano whose 1984 Central Saint Martin's final show Les Incroyables was pure New Romantic.

Street Style

Flamboyant colours, silks, furs and velvets, theatrical costumes and full make-up were de rigeur for the New Romantics' gender-fluid subculture.

ACID HOUSE /
RAVE CULTURE

In the summer of 1988, a new subculture emerged which
changed the social landscape of the UK. As with other
youth-driven movements there was immediate concern
that acid house would bring about the moral downfall
of Britain's young, especially given its link with the new
drug on the block, ecstasy. However, the moral panic was
ill-founded, with ecstasy instead launching a wave of love
and euphoria that scooped up whole groups into joyous,
hands-in-the-air unity.

Born in the frenzied nightclubs of Great Britain, notably Manchester's The Haçienda and London's Shoom (the birthplace of the iconic smiley face logo), acid house's music and dance scene soon spread to large illegal raves, planned on the hoof at disused warehouses across the land. As the DJ Sasha told the *Guardian* in 2014: "Most of the fun of the night was the chase, trying to find the warehouse while evading the police."

Where punks were angry and aggressive, and other subcultures political and anti-establishment, ravers were content to keep partying, no thinking required. The loved-up vibe had much in common with hippies, and social boundaries melted away in a positive embrace of multiculturalism.

Rave fashion soon evolved to suit the heat that long hours of dancing generated. Outfits consisted of baggy trousers, sweatpants or dungarees, with logo T-shirts featuring slogans including "Pump up the Jam", "Trip with Acid" or just a huge bright-yellow smiley face. Cycling shorts or crazily patterned Bermudas were popular and feet were clad in trainers or comfy Clarks Wallabees shoes. Bandanas and bucket hats absorbed the sweat, and neon glow sticks, whistles and sunglasses were essential accessories. As acid house became more fashion-focused, batik-print hoodies and trousers appeared as partygoers returned to London from Ibiza, and Vivienne Westwood cashed in on the trend, designing Care Bear and acid-print T-shirts.

Acid house lasted into the early 1990s. Rave culture only truly died out in 1994 with the Criminal Justice and Public Order Act, which gave police the power to shut down open-air gatherings.

Ravers outside The Trip at the Astoria in 1988, the birthplace of the House music revolution.

Street Style

GOTH

Goth came into being as part of gothic rock, first noted in 1981 when the UK rock magazine *Sounds* published a piece titled "The face of Punk Gothique", alluding to the macabre-obsessed subculture as the next big thing.

Bands including the Sisters of Mercy, the Cure and Adam and the Ants were all part of the goth scene, although before it was named, artists including the Damned and Siouxsie and the Banshees had started exhibiting emotional angst, dark themes and androgyny.

With fashion too, there had been a lean into a darkly feminine aesthetic that included plenty of velvet, draped sheer fabrics and fishnet tights. This soon evolved into what is considered the signature goth look, which includes long flowing skirts and voluminous tops with batwing sleeves, leather, velvet, corsetry and Victorian accessories such as lace gloves. An obsession with the undead and supernatural saw occult symbols such as pentagrams worn as jewellery. Make-up was a huge part of the image, with whitened skin, dark eyeliner and lipstick, and black painted nails on men and women alike.

Goth club nights took off in the early 1980s with the legendary Batcave launching in 1982 at Soho's Gargoyle Club where regulars included Nick Cave, Robert Smith and Siouxsie Sioux. The fashion subculture has far from disappeared from London's streets with Camden Market still a mecca for goth fashion.

A group of 80s goths wearing the typical black draped
Victoriana-inspired velvet and lace outfits.

Overleaf: Olli Wisdom and Jonny Slut from glam-goth band Specimen
pose theatrically for a photoshoot at London's Batcave club night, 1984.

Street Style

SLOANE RANGER

The notorious term for upper-class London socialites was coined in 1975 by Peter York and Ann Barr in an article for *Harpers & Queen*. But it was not until 1982, when the pair published *The Official Sloane Ranger Handbook*, that fascination with the speech, dress and mannerisms of this privileged tribe of youngsters hit the mainstream.

The reason for this was, of course, Princess Diana. The "Supersloane", as York and Barr dubbed her, had recently married Prince Charles and the resulting frenzy of attention made the look a worldwide phenomenon.

The style was a cross between country casual and formal tradition. Barbour jackets, "pie-crust" collars and pastel cashmere twinsets were accessorized by pearl necklaces, velvet headbands and ballet flats. But as York pointed out in an interview with the *Guardian* in 2020, unlike other fashion subcultures who deliberately chose to dress a certain way to belong, the Sloane "...evolved from a particular kind of parent and their dress code, and a particular kind of schooling and that dress code." The trend has experienced a revival over the last few years thanks to shows like *The Crown*.

One of the earliest shots of Diana outside her London flat in 1980. The young aristocrat epitomizes the Sloane Ranger look.

Overleaf: A typically decadent 1980s scene from Tramp, the Mayfair nightclub beloved of the Sloane Ranger set. Founder Johnny Gold lies on the polished bar as the club's glamorous high-society clientele relax, drinking and smoking around him.

MODERN
STREET STYLE

Thanks to TikTok and other sites, street style and alternative fashion subcultures have become thoroughly democratized. Goth and punk are seeing a Gen Z revival, e-girls and e-boys crowd the internet, and even Scene kids from the early noughties are back. Fashion is taking note, with top designers peppering their collections with subculture references. What started in London, and other cities, in the 1960s has finally reached every corner of the globe.

The adage goes that there is nothing new in fashion, and customizing outfits for a unique look is typical of street style, pictured here during London Fashion Week in 2019.

Gender-fluid street style has become increasingly common – as seen here with a pink frilled dress worn over athleisure black T-shirt and shorts.

A vibrant retro look made up of green dungarees and a 1980s-style double-breasted, square-shouldered check jacket paired with round glasses. The camera slung round the neck is a must-have fashion week accessory.

Street style outside yuhan wang during Fashion Week 2021. The contrast between the feminine pink dress and iconic Doc Marten shoes is classic London.

SHOPPING GUIDE

Department stores:
Liberty, Regent Street
Selfridges, Oxford Street
Harvey Nichols, Knightsbridge
Harrods, Brompton Road

British Designers:
Stella McCartney, Old Bond Street
Alexander McQueen, Old Bond Street
Burberry, Regent Street
Margaret Howell, Wigmore Street
Vivienne Westwood, Conduit Street

Shoes:
John Lobb, St James's Street
Churches, New Bond Street

Clothes Emporiums/selected areas:
Dover Street Market
Redchurch Street
Borough Yards
Coal Drop Yard
Lamb's Conduit Street
Seven Dials/Covent Garden

Vintage stores/areas:

Portobello Road – especially 282 Portobello and Found and Vision
Brick Lane – especially Serotonin Vintage
Ladbroke Grove
Storm in a Teacup, Kingsland Road
The Market Cartel, Amhurst Road
Beyond Retro, Argyll Street
Paper Dress Vintage, Mare Street

Fabric and Haberdashery stores/areas:

Goldhawk Road
Berwick Street
Cloth House, Royal College Street
Joel & Son Fabrics, Church Street
MacCulloch & Wallis, Poland Street
V V Rouleaux, Marylebone Lane
Village Haberdashery, Heritage Lane

Sale stores and sample sales:

Margaret Howell, Margaret Street
Arlettie, Margaret Street
The Music Rooms, South Molton Lane
The Box, Ram Place
Hackney Walk, Morning Lane

Markets:

Princess May Car Boot Sale, Barrett's Grove
Battersea Car Boot, Battersea Park Road
Alfies Antique Market, Lisson Grove
Hammersmith Vintage Fair, Kensington High Street

iNDEX

CREDITS

The publishers would like to thank the following sources for their kind permission to reproduce the pictures in this book.

Alamy: dpa picture alliance 64, 146-147; Keystone Press 104; PA Images 50, 106; Pictorial Press Ltd 27; Retro AdArchives 37; Reuters 72; Shawshots 14; TT News Agency 138; Victor Watts 150-151

Bridgeman Images: © Malcolm English. All Rights Reserved 2022 134-135

Kerry Taylor Auctions: 33, 58

Getty Images: Pool Arnal/Pat 47; Janette Beckman 49; David M. Benett 89, 117, 118; Bentley Archive/Popperfoto 107; Edward Berthelot 93, 153; Bettman 18; Giancarlo Botti 23; Dominique Charriau 69; David Corio 45; Dove/Stringer 100; Michel Dufour 71; Erica Echenberg/Contributor 136; Estrop 78; Evening Standard/Stringer 133; Express Newspapers/Stringer 103; Terry Fincher/Stringer 129b; Jeremy Fletcher 130; Tim Graham 110, 111; Caroline Greville-Morris 141; Dave Hogan 115, 122r; Hulton Archive/Stringer 41; The Image Gate/Stringer 90; Images Press 60; Keystone/Stringer 102; Gie Knaeps 109; Catherine McGann 63; Terry McGinnis 119; Mike Marsland 68; John D Mchugh 86; Michael Ochs Archives/

Stringer 105; Neil Mockford 155; Frank Monaco 129t; David Montgomery 29; Antonio de Moraes Barros Filho 83; John Phillips/BFC 81; Phillips/Stringer 13, 24; Hugo Philpott 70; Popperfoto 17, 99, 127; Princess Diana Archive/Stringer 54, 149; Steve Rapport 112; David Redfern 101; Bertrand Rindoff Petroff 61; Peter Ruck/Stringer 34; Pascal Le Segretain 122l; Kirstin Sinclair 120; Jeff Spicer/BFC 94; John Stoddart/Popperfoto 57; Michael Stroud/Stringer 131; Karwai Tang 123; Victor Virgile 66-67; Justin de Villeneuve/Hulton Archive 28

Norman Parkinson: Iconic Images 7, 8

Shutterstock: ANL 31, 114; Aflo 154; Brendan Beirne 113; Richard Braine/Pymca 137; Business Collection 53; David Dagley 43; Charles Knight 77; Mark Large/ANL 84; Elisa Leonelli 44; Feri Lukas 145; Frank Micelotta 75; Silvia Olsen 152; Gianni Penati/Condé Nast 38

Universal Images Group: Marcus Graham/Avalon 142

Every effort has been made to acknowledge correctly and contact the source and/or copyright holder of each picture and Welbeck Publishing apologises for any unintentional errors or omissions, which will be corrected in future editions of this book.